Gifts
from the
Garden

If you are a gardener, or if you simply wish for a moment's respite to immerse yourself in nature and the mysteries of life, you will find here a willing muse and a kindred spirit.

Gifts
from the
Garden

Carol Siyahi Hicks

Printed 2012 in the United States of America.

Paperback: ISBN: 978-0-615-53968-3

Sea Eagle Press

When I was a child, I watched my mother escape to her garden. There she could be alone and at peace, surrounded by beauty. I think she found her sense of wonder there... and it was a place where mine grew. This book is dedicated to all who love gardens and whose hearts hold a certain sense of wonder – and to my mother, who at 94 still has hers firmly intact.

Foreword

Throughout the ages, gardens have been at once an outlet for creative expression, an intoxication of the senses, a battleground between living and dying, and a respite for the spirit. Francis Bacon said that even "God Almighty first planted a garden."

Gardens provide metaphors for living. In gardens are all the stages of life, laid out amid the change of seasons and the rise and flow of time.

Truly gardens are vibrant with life and death. Yet despite the daily struggle for survival that they represent for the creatures and flora that inhabit them, they have the potential to be places of remarkable beauty, human reflection and renewal, and infinite spiritual solace. They are a collection of life forces growing in the space between the grit of Earth and the expansive dreaming of the sky.

"The earth held its
breath for spring."

The Weight and Levity of Snow:
Living in the Moment while Waiting for Spring

GOLDENROD LANGUISHED BENEATH THE WEIGHT OF
SNOW. It bent toward an earth hard with winter and
waiting. The earth held its breath for spring. But the land
was glowing in its ghostly garb, draped over the dried,
brown stalks of my flower garden and the fields beyond,
stalks transfixed, frozen in form by the frosts of late fall
and early winter.

My cross-country skis bit the crust of the snow
on the path my husband, George, cut with his John
Deere tractor, past the garden and through the once-lush
greenness of the grasses and prairie plants in the back acres
of our property. I watched the frozen forms of the plants,
once alive with purples and yellows, whites and golds,
browns and greens. Now there was only brown and white.
Form and purity. Earth and water. Substance and air. Life
and death. This moment.

I always have loved snow days in Ohio, especially because we have so precious few of them. When the snow would come in plenitude – more than a dusting, enough on which to ski – I would feel unbridled joy. I found I would do almost anything to grab hold of the moment and rush outside with my twenty-year-old pair of skis to kick and glide my way across our five acres of land. I would go in the dark if I had to, get up early to ski before work, or take off from my job to spend time playing in the snow. Because later that day, or tomorrow, it all could be gone. Snow in Ohio, if you love it, forces you to live in the moment. It is a gift of fullness sprung from meagerness.

So round and round I skied. First along the fence line with our neighbor who has the horses. Then along the boundary with the neighbor at a distance who has the disturbingly blue house in an otherwise earth-toned landscape. Then along the fence between us and the neighbor with the goats – three or four varieties of curious, bearded, and horned fellows with their watchful eyes and rounded bellies. Finally up a little hill and along the west edge of the pond George dug a few years back with his tractor. And then round again.

It was not unusual for me to round the field for an hour at a time. I usually ended up by taking several runs down the larger hill beside our house, down toward the pond, narrowly missing its icy surface with its half-frozen fish waiting like the earth for spring. I could glide almost to the barn at the north side of our property, having started from the southernmost end. I marked my ski tracks to try for progressively farther finishes. It was a contest I had with myself, finding ways to increase speed, momentum, and ultimately distance, marking the end point of my final glide.

And when I had spent all my time and energy, I climbed in herringbone form back up the hill to deposit myself sweaty and exhausted, but strangely invigorated, in my home that opened to the land all white and full of form and sky and light.

"Gardens can become a lasting
obsession."

A Strange Delight

GARDENS ARE A STRANGE DELIGHT. They express the creative spirit, teach lessons about life, refresh the mind, and enchant the soul. They also can become a lasting obsession.

Since I became "a gardener," I cannot walk through mine without bending to pluck an errant weed or an unwanted beetle or earwig. Or mentally rearranging plants. Or worrying about a failed flower or a drooping bush. It is rather like having many children waiting to be tended, kept healthy, encouraged, and admired.

Although I frequently have put in more than fifty hours at my place of work, I still have managed as much as ten or fifteen hours a week in my garden during the height of the growing season. Needless to say, in gardening season housework suffers. But then, George and I spend most of our time outdoors when weather permits. We are not creatures who can stay indoors happily when the delights of sunshine, breezes, an ever-changing sky, wildlife, and gardens beckon. So it was easy to justify to myself time spent with my fingers dug into the earth.

I found success in gardening innocently enough. I started by planting a few flowers here and there to decorate my new home in the country and my new marriage. It seemed simple at first. Then something wonderful happened. What I planted not only grew, but flourished and became beautiful. I was amazed. I had thought I wasn't any good at gardening. After all, more of my houseplants had died than survived in the past. And before being married to George, when I lived in my home in a nearby village, I had gardened beneath a canopy of ginkgoes, an oak hundreds of years old, and a huge elm to ill effect. I planted. I watered. I watched my plants struggle and lag. I fought with the spindly little fellows to no avail and finally concluded that I wasn't much of a gardener.

And then I moved to George's home in the country. Suddenly I had acres of untended land, plenty of sunshine, and good soil, further enriched with manure from a neighbor's barn.

And wonder of wonders: what I planted didn't just grow, it thrived. And quite unexpectedly I became a "gardener." And so a delightful addiction began.

*　　*　　*

It is easy for me to understand – now – how people can have such passion for their gardens. I never fully understood it until I had some success with my own. It is a creative undertaking that requires the ability to envision possibility. It takes patience, because nothing you plant will be as it will ten years from now or even five or one. You must be willing to wait. And watch. And hope.

"It is as if your innermost self
emerges from hibernation
to stand in the presence of
life opening impatiently
around you. The spring bulbs
can hardly wait to leave the
underground as they tear up
through the soil and explode
into the warming air."

The Intrinsic Readiness of Spring

SPRING WAS LONG THIS YEAR. In Ohio spring frequently has lasted only two or three weeks. This time, however, the cool to moderate temperatures and the rain held on well into June. The spring flowers bloomed exuberantly, and my cool-temperature-loving pansies had an unusually extended season.

The coolness kept the mosquitoes at bay and delayed the planting of tomato and pepper plants. The weeds, however, grew in abundance, as did the grass. At times it seemed as if all George and I did was pull weeds and mow grass. But it was wonderful to have this long period of gentle temperatures and lush, spring growth.

Later, because of the protracted spring, the summer flowers started blooming while the spring ones hung on. Daylilies mingled with pansies, hollyhock with flowering sage, flowering yucca with chrysanthemum – a chaotic mix of seasons colliding in my Ohio garden.

There is something about the start of spring that

stirs the soul. It is as if your innermost self emerges from hibernation to stand in the presence of life opening impatiently around you. The spring bulbs can hardly wait to leave the underground as they tear up through the soil and explode into the warming air. The grass starts to become that color we call "spring green," like no other green I've seen outside of the British Isles except at this time of year.

The trees and bushes with their tight buds ache now to expand into their new foliage – and frequently do so too soon. But for the plants that wait, oh what a joy they are in their young foliage, all yellow-green and fresh. There is an intrinsic readiness about spring that comes from long waiting, a readiness that we humans experience as well. This feeling, it seems to me, is part of our deep, human need for change. We are at our best – or worst, if this is our inclination – when we are responding to the unexpected. It calls up something firmly instinctual to which our whole system – physical, emotional, and spiritual – responds. The shift of seasons forces change upon us humans who tend to resist the very thing that enlivens and expands us.

And then there is the simple enjoyment of spring's special mixture of sensual pleasures. The scent of lilacs behind the house. The brush of a gentle breeze against the skin. The intensity of color in the rows of tulips and in the lawn with its haunting green spilling down the hill toward the pond dazzling under a sunlit and lavishly blue sky.

"You have to be willing to just plunge in, dirt up to your elbows, and see what happens."

On Being Willing to Fail

IF YOU WANT TO SUCCEED AT GARDENING, you have to be willing to fail.

Great gardening requires a certain boldness. It helps to be open to the nontraditional plant, an unconventional border, or an uneven arrangement. You need a taste for the unexpected and a touch of fearlessness about the unknown.

You have to be willing to just plunge in, dirt up to your elbows, and see what happens. It helps if you like surprises – because your garden always will surprise you. Sometimes the unexpected is to your liking, and sometimes it is not.

I have lost the better part of two hundred and fifty great, fat spring bulbs shipped all the way from Holland to assure the best pedigree. I had spent weeks planning their layout around my former house in town. The blooms were going to be magnificent in spring. I had calculated where to plant which cycle of tulip, lily, narcissus, daffodil, woods hyacinth, anemone, and snowdrop so I would have bulbs in bloom at all times from March through June. I spent numerous fall days digging up garden space and planting the bulbs three to eight inches deep (depending upon the type) in the soil that I dutifully mixed with bulb food and other nutrients. I even sprinkled red pepper sauce on them to discourage squirrels and other rodents. I covered the bulbs and mulched them well. Then I sat back and waited out the long, winter months until spring. I told all my friends and neighbors about the planting and my hopes for the next season. I joked with them about how I had put in so many spring bulbs that I envisioned them raising my house toward the heavens as the March sun warmed the earth and began to release the plants from the bulbs.

The first year I had a nice display of color. But perhaps only half of the plants came up that first year and maybe a third the next. I later found that the squirrels, despite my peppering, indeed had discovered the delectable bulbs and had made a royal feast of them. I fantasized that the squirrels were Mexican and that they hotly relished my well-peppered plantings.

I was devastated. Despite all my planning, work, and expense, I had failed at having a spring extravaganza of color. I had been outwitted by rodents. But oh, if I had succeeded, what a wonder that would have been!

You have to be willing to try again, and if your new effort fails, try yet again. Modest efforts yield modest results, so you need to be willing to dare. It's a lot like life. It's especially hard to be public with your dreams. Along with going public goes a declaration of commitment to what you've imagined. Then if you fail, you fail publicly. And no one likes to fail – especially not in full view of others. But the longer you garden and the longer you live, you learn to mind your failures less and less. You develop a certain grace about them. They become your scars, your little badges of courage. You know that at least you tried. At least you dared.

"If you plan for a little shade
in places where you best can sit
and enjoy what at times can be
an immodest display of color
and texture, you can find gentle
moments of relief for both body
and spirit in the excesses
of summer."

Summer Dreaming

IT SEEMS TO ME THAT WE SIMPLY MELD INTO SUMMER.
The entrance of summer carries none of the heraldry of the
other seasons – no coming to life in spring, no wakening
to cool and the intensification of fall, no shock of cold with
the onslaught of winter. We simply drift into summer, roll
along on the lethargy that accompanies the heat.

I always feel a certain letdown when the energizing
cool breaks and the hot, humid weather begins. As I
sweat from exertion in the hot temperatures, I can feel
the vitality drain from my body. We are, after all, mostly
water. Our very cells seem to cry out as they are milked of
their life-giving fluids. My mind becomes as sluggish as my
body, and it isn't long before I have to go inside to snatch a
break from the stress of the heat.

Plants, even trees, suffer as well when the
temperatures remain high without the relief of rain and
cooling fronts. Plants can collapse in the heat like a person
hit by heat stroke. And, like people, sometimes they don't

revive. Potted plants are the most vulnerable, as they cannot draw on little bits of moisture in the surrounding soil or from deeper in the earth. Also highly susceptible are plants in full sun that are close to cement patios or other reflective surfaces. But any extended period of intense heat can bleed moisture from the air and rob plants first of their beauty, then of their good health, and ultimately of their life.

So when we leave home for a week or more, I rely on neighbors to watch over my plants and give them a little water now and then to tide them over until we return.

I have found, too, that it is best when you plant to not push the limits of how much sun or shade a particular plant can bear if you want to have the most beautiful summer gardens. The combination of sunshine, nutrients, and the moisture you assure can make for the fullest floral displays of the year. And if you plan for a little shade in places where you best can sit and enjoy what at times can be an immodest display of color and texture, you can find gentle moments of relief for both body and spirit in the excesses of summer.

"A seed is a delicate and
mysterious thing."

The Sublime Nature of Seeds

YOU CAN ENJOY INSTANT GRATIFICATION when you take home a young plant from the nursery and put it in your garden. Immediately you get exactly what you expected and can enjoy it on the spot.

But a seed…that is a different matter.

A seed is a delicate and mysterious thing. You may purchase seeds or harvest them from last year's crop. You have to imagine the full-grown plant when you bury the seed, and you must sow it just right. It should not be planted too deep or too shallow. It ought to be in the proper soil and the right distance between the rows – or between clusters if you're not a row gardener. You need to pat the soil down over the seed, but not too firmly. Then you should water it gently and mark your seedbeds. If you fail to, the seeds quickly will become lost in weeds, or you will forget which seed is which. Then you must keep watering…and you wait.

Seeds are especially good at growing patience. I

am not the world's most patient person, but I am learning it with the help of seeds. Some seem to take forever to sprout. These seeds – like children – are the greatest patience teachers.

Recently I put in a row of Gloriosa Daisy seeds harvested from a magnificent plant I bought from a local nursery halfway through last summer. I kept the seeds, as I so loved these daisies. I planted their seeds, tapped them down properly, and marked the row with sticks. I watered and waited, watered and waited. Nothing. Ah, the seeds are not good, I thought. Nothing will happen. But I kept watering. (I may not be the most patient person, but I am persistent.) I watered. I watched. I waited some more. Then one day weeks after planting, I saw the tiniest grey-green leaves. I had to look more than once to assure myself they were even there. They were that small. But there was a whole row of them, barely peeking out of the soil. I danced for joy in my vegetable garden with its little row of Gloriosa Daisies-in-waiting. I could hardly believe it. Who would imagine that such enormous daisies would rise from these little leaves, scarcely larger than pinheads!

Every day I walked down to the vegetable garden to look at them. I measured their progress, which was ever so slow. But they were steadily growing. In two or three weeks they might be large enough to thin and transplant. Already I was thinking about the different places I could plant them. I wanted them everywhere – those large, brown faces with their sunny nest of yellow-gold petals looking back at me all through the summer. How exciting – I could hardly wait!

Other seeds appear to spring up overnight. Green bean seeds are like that. In what seems like a week, they may burst through the soil with nearly full-grown leaves – heave up out of the dirt like an eruption of lava, breaking the earth open as they gasp for air. In no time they can be ready for thinning and transplanting. They are easy to grow and almost instantly satisfying.

My zinnia seeds were a mixed bag this year. I had purchased a package of giant zinnia seeds this year and sown them on the edge of my vegetable garden. I thought that a splash of color down the hill from my main garden and close to our pond would delight and give me plenty of flowers for picking. About a foot away, I sowed another row of zinnias, these harvested from last year's smaller and brightly colored plants that I nurtured. But these seeds did poorly. Few sprouted. Fortunately my store-bought seeds were sufficiently prolific to cover the two rows I'd planned.

When I was at Butchart Gardens outside Victoria, Canada, I bought trailing, hanging-basket flower seeds. I opened the packet this spring and found six tiny envelopes inside the outer one. Most had names I didn't recognize – and there were no pictures on the inner packets. I opened one of the seed containers and found such tiny seeds that I could scarcely see them. I decided I should plant them first in pots, or they would be lost in no time. I sprinkled three varieties over very fine soil and covered them with just a dusting of earth. I watered them oh-so-carefully. Two of the three began to show themselves in a week – the third may have been harmed by the rain. They were such small, spindly little creatures, I could hardly wait to see what they would become when they were all grown up. They were my mystery seeds. If I was lucky, I could plant them in hanging baskets and have lovely, trailing flowers intermingle with the more upright, previously established ones.

These might have been my mystery plants, but in truth, all seeds to me are mysterious. How they sprout, how they grow, their tentativeness and their cycles, what they will look like, what they can become – all are mystifying to me. All life evolves from some type of seed. How it knows what to become – that a bean never grows up to be a zinnia, or a Gloriosa Daisy seed never becomes a tomato – is amazing to me. It is the secret of life, packaged in a small jacket of a shell, released to become something wonderful when it blends with the nourishment of earth and the life-giving touch of water and sunshine.

A seed is a truly splendid thing. Sublime. Sensual even.

"The fragileness of life
is everywhere in a garden. It is
in the silky blossoms torn by
wind and insects. It is in the
grasshopper, once strong and
now food for bluegills. It is
in the memory of the seasons
and the knowledge that
everything changes."

Fall Migrations
*Be still and listen. The air is alive
with expectation.*

A LONE, PERFECT, GIANT WHITE CLEMATIS BLOSSOM
radiated from the withering green of its tangled vines.
It was a burst of beauty from a plant that I had been
considering replacing the next year. The plant had had a
disappointing lack of flowers. I had spent half of a precious
summer day, weaving a web of string for it to branch out
from the trellis it had outgrown. I had nourished the plant
regularly with a fertilizer made to promote blooms and
kept its head in the sun and its feet cool and moist, as it
likes. But for all this effort, we had only four blossoms all
summer, each of which was eaten by grasshoppers within a
day of flowering.

One morning I killed a grasshopper that was eating
my climbing rose and that was preparing to attack the
remaining clematis flower. Not to waste a life, even that of

this unwelcome and sorry creature, I carried his smashed body down to our pond. I stood on the dock jutting out over the dozen or so feet of water depth here and watched the bluegills line up in rows and wait for me to cast the bug's dead body out across the air and into the pond. The grasshopper barely hit the water when the bluegills attacked. They carried it beneath the water's surface and pulled it apart. They feasted on the insect stuffed with leaves and rose petals.

*   *   *

The fragileness of life is everywhere in a garden. It is in the silky blossoms torn by wind and insects. It is in the grasshopper, once strong and now food for bluegills. It is in the memory of the seasons and the knowledge that everything changes. "The moment" is all in a garden. And nothing lasts forever in life as well, except love, honor, and sacrifice.

*   *   *

The flowers in my garden that had survived several light frosts this fall had come back radiant beyond imagining. My yellow rose bush, which struggled mightily through the heat of summer, now was rich with green and new, red leaves and the firm buds that soon would burst with yellow perfection.

The purple yarrow had begun a new cycle of flowering. The purple-centered, white daisies had taken on new life, and the gazania, which had been disappointing all summer, now exploded with striking yellow and dark-accented blooms along the edge of my garden.

A few marigolds, miniature orange zinnias, and blue and purple pansies remained – and, of course, the hardy mums. The mums were past their prime, but their rusts and too-bright purples and yellows still dominated. It was interesting how these colors and the blues were hardier than the pinks and whites of summer. A single, purple coneflower stood above the dried, browned, and spent coneflowers with which it was intermingled. Although seemingly devoid of life, the dried flowers' centers held seeds that the birds would harvest when winter left little else on which to feed.

*   *   *

I picked the last of the basil today. I pulled the plants from the earth and carefully trimmed away frost-blackened sections of the leaves. I even removed the soft, green seedpods to use in my last batch of pesto for the year. I found myself wishing I had brought the plants in before the cold had hit. I would have had two to three batches instead of this partial one. But I took great care to retrieve all I could, as there is nothing that so brings back the summer and enlivens cold evenings as a serving of homemade pesto, made with basil picked fresh from the garden and frozen until it is ready to be warmed and eaten in the dead of winter.

*   *   *

So much waited to be done this time of year. There was the clearing of the vegetable garden, the scattering of the remaining, ruined fruit to reseed the garden for next year, and the gathering of tomato and pepper cages. I had to cut back the rose bushes, daisies, hollyhock stalks, and the black-eyed Susan. I brought the plants indoors that we wanted to winter over – the large, potted hibiscus bushes, containers of healthy, well-developed geranium, the bougainvillea, a few favorite green plants, and the exotic Mandevilla vine with its summer-blooming, large, pink trumpet flowers.

As I cut back dead and dried flowers, I noted how many young, green hollyhock plants dotted the eastern edge of my garden. Observing such an abundance of small plants, I rejoiced at the thought of so many grown and blooming ones we seemed destined to have next year. Would they be the very dark, red single flowers that the hollyhock plants put forth this year, or would they be the pale pink, green, and yellow-white singles that were so delicate and special in last year's garden? We would have to wait until next summer to see. I so love the anticipation. But whichever kind they would be, they would be plentiful!

*   *   *

Hollyhocks are nostalgic for me. I remember them lined up along the north side of my childhood home on Long Island. I used to love the varieties of "singles" and "doubles" that appeared year after year and the strange creatures the plants hosted. I remember watching once in utter fascination, a battle between a praying mantis and a large, fat, green, garden spider. It was a long standoff, but the praying mantis finally won.

These plants nourished my early entrepreneurial fantasies. As the hollyhocks produced the pods ripe with dried seeds, I, as a grade-school child, would harvest them. I would place the seeds in envelopes labeled with the type of hollyhock they were. Then I would walk door to door in our neighborhood and sell the seeds for two cents an envelope. I would make enough to squander on chocolates at the nearby drugstore or on ice cream from the Good Humor man. They taught me how to work for what I wanted. Gardens hold many lessons, even for the very young.

*   *   *

The day was crisp and vibrant with sun. It was a welcome change from the cold, biting dampness and dreary skies of the last few days.

With the ending of summer, the sounds of the garden had undergone a transformation. There was none of the whirring, buzzing, and droning of insects that dominated just a few weeks ago. The air had become strangely quiet, except for periodic sounds from birds and a few hardier breeds of insects – ladybugs and grasshoppers in particular. From time to time, I could hear insects alight on nearby leaves and the busy sounds of birds that had not migrated south – the doves, robins, cardinals, grackles, sparrows, woodpeckers, and hawks. I was aware of the strengthening wind and the crackle of dried leaves as they let loose from their branches, the leaves rustling against one another as they fell, dancing, twirling their way to earth.

As the sun started to set beyond the fields behind our house and the soon-to-be-glowing pond, I heard the faint honking of Canada geese traveling in formation across the reddening sky. They flew every day over our garden and house – each morning and evening. I always rushed to see them. I saw a primitiveness in their patterns, the gutturalness of their honking, the drumming of the air under their wings. As they passed overhead, they produced a vibration that was haunting and beckoned.

The geese reminded me of the patterns that come from instinct. Those ancient forces born into the very memory of our bodies' cells. They are like an internal tide ebbing and flowing with the force of our primitive pasts. No species escapes them. They protect, guide, and baffle us. They are a force like the surge of the surf, from which we sometimes cannot pull ourselves free.

*   *   *

This day was special, not only for its brilliance and ampleness of experience, but also because it was the first day since spring that we had not been on daylight saving time. We dutifully turned back our clocks the previous night before we went to bed. This day we had an extra hour to run, gather the last of the garden, and fret over how to build a cold frame under the gazebo before winter. But I would miss that extra hour of daylight, that precious light in which to drive home from work and savor the day briefly before fixing dinner. It was barely five o'clock as I sat writing. But the sun was descending rapidly, angling light low and echoing through the golds and pinks of the maple trees that were sheltered from the wind by a row of mature white pines. The setting light came to rest on the surface of the pond, now reflecting mirrorlike the warm vibrancy of the fall sun. The rich roses and golds glided along the pond and reached out to the sky, dazzling against the approaching chill of the night.

*   *   *

In areas undisturbed by George's tractor, the long, low light of this fall afternoon revealed spiders' intricate web-weaving everywhere over the surface of the grass and long strands of spider-silk flying from nearly every branch. How was it that I never saw this before? How did I not know how busy these creatures are, spinning beauty with death in a secret world just below the surface of our awareness?

*   *   *

I took a walk in the field at the back of our property. The Queen Anne's lace and goldenrod had gone to seed. The milkweed pods had broken open. The pods' silky tufts had traveled and caught on the dried stalks of the goldenrod. A pair of mockingbirds scolded from a branch above the tin shed that sheltered my garden pots and cages and that now vibrated in the wind. The racehorse in the neighbors' field on the other side of us from the neighbors with the goats, watched me with interest. He was curious, but shy. I broke off some grass to coax him, but he turned and walked slowly away.

I had better luck, however, with the six grazing goats. I gained their interest by offering long, slender stalks from our field. A brown goat with white on the top of his head and sides went first for the bait. But shortly, the largest of the white goats, the one with the very long horns, took the weeds while nudging the others away. I petted him on the nose as he nibbled at the greenery with surprising delicacy. The goats' eyes were curious, but not very soulful or keen with intelligence. Their beards were long and played with a passing breeze.

A mockingbird, sitting high on a branch near the edge of our property, projected a lovely singsong of considerable variety and complexity. A cow groaned some distance away. It was a low and ample sound over the metallic noise of a tractor rising in a neighboring field and the distant scream of a car speeding along a nearby road.

As I walked back toward the house to prepare dinner, I heard branches rustling in the wind and a plopping sound as a slender bass broke the surface of the pond in search of an insect.

*　　*　　*

The sky was that crisp blue that bright sunshine brings on a day in late fall. It was breezy too. The wind created small waves on the surface of the pond and lifted the branches of the large white pines separating the pond from the hill above. There the gazebo, the house, and my garden nestle.

The wind shook leaves in the trees, rattled the dried

flowers and bushes, and scurried along the brick steps and patio. A hawk drifted silently overhead. Ladybugs flew and landed everywhere. One bit me on the ankle as I worked to clear dead flowers from the garden.

Along the south side of the gazebo, under which George had built cold frames, we had planted lettuce, spinach, and herbs for winter picking. For insulation, we packed plastic garbage sacks with leaves and banked them around the cold frame's base under the gazebo floorboards.

The insects were busy this day – not just the ladybugs, but flies and gnats as well. Just a few flowers remained, though, including a small number of the star-shaped Sweet Autumn Clematis blooms that climbed along the brick wall outside my kitchen window. Pale yellow, almost white, daisylike mums halfway down the hill toward the pond were backlit by the sun and were almost translucent. They were long on the stalk and had fallen over from the weight of their prolific blooms. These mums were so much more strikingly beautiful where the light shone through, than from the other side where the direct light flattened and stole their beauty. Or so it seemed from my perch just above and beside them, there on the pink, granite rock on which I sat inhaling the freshness of the air. I watched, too, the nectar-loving insects nuzzle the flowers' centers – these insects included bees, wasps, hornets, and even flies.

Queen Anne's lace rolled in the wind beside the leavings of the vegetable garden. The last of the peppers, small and shriveled from freezing and thawing, hung like dusty, old Christmas lights from the dried plants. Dead tomato vines had fallen from their wire supports and collapsed onto the boards put down for walking and for weed control.

As I gazed at the spent vegetable garden from my stone seat, the wind gently drummed my ear. The air, almost whistling, traveled across the field and over the pond, then through the white pines like surf along the shore. A dog barked a farm or two away.

I got up, walked down to the pond, and sat on the end of the pier. The bluegills gathered, waiting for food. Even the large, shy catfish came to look, wait, and beg. The ending of fall meant there were few bugs or baby fish to eat, and certainly no tadpoles. The fish were hungry and preparing to hibernate. They would have liked a little more food to fatten them and keep them warm over the winter.

The heads of the dried cattails had turned fluffy. Their seeds waited to catch the wind, land, and propagate.

The neighbors' goats grazed among the weeds beside our fence. Their heads were down as they ate for the coming cold and only occasionally glanced up from their task. In the same neighbors' yard, a deciduous cedar tree – unlike its more usual evergreen cousin – was covered in brown needles. Soon they would fall and carpet the ground like a virgin dropping her dress on her wedding night, dying to her old life and being born to her new. A few maples around us continued to hold their golden leaves. Most, however, had shed them. The leaves rolled around and scattered across the lawn between our land and our neighbors' and out toward the field. The ferns from the asparagus plants on the boundary line had born bright, red berries. The plants had toppled over from the weight of their long stems, and the berries hovered just barely above the ground. In the chill of winter, the birds would find them and rejoice.

Similarly, it so often is the case that we discover bright little nuggets of life waiting quietly for us in the midst of dark moments. When hope seems most lost to us, we often find it. It may come as a call from a friend, a gesture of encouragement from a colleague, a smile from a stranger, the most incredible sunset tearing through seams of heavy, rain-laden clouds, or a lovely little red berry on an asparagus plant, just waiting to be plucked by a hungry bird in the harshness of winter.

"'Gardeners are beggars,' my
mother always said."

Gardens and Neighbors

GARDENS AND THE SHRUBS AND TREES THAT PUNCTUATE them mark boundaries of many kinds. They define property. They screen you from unsightly views. They can reduce noise and help shield you from the elements. They describe your personal style and express your creativity and sensibility. They beckon or they exclude. "Good fences make good neighbors," Robert Frost wrote. And so it is with gardens.

If you have neighbors who are gardeners, gardens also can collapse boundaries and provide a joyful way to bond. It is especially pleasant to be out in your garden, while your neighbor and friend is in hers or his and chatter back and forth while pulling weeds, planting starts, or harvesting flowers or vegetables.

Neighbors can be great for swapping plants or rocks and adding to the diversity of your garden. "Gardeners are beggars," my mother always said. So true! More than half of my current, large flower garden has come from friends and former neighbors. They have given me my white and bearded iris, forget-me-not, pink yarrow, yellow daylily, black-eyed Susan, white and yellow daisy, pink daisy-mums, hosta, sedum, Vinca, and most of my herbs: cilantro, basil, sage, parsley, oregano, thyme, and mint.

You may trade landscaping ideas, stories about gardening, and moral support. You can help one another lift heavy shrubs, trees, and rocks. Or you just can work together on one another's weeding and planting, swapping time and companionship.

We even have had garden parties with neighbors and other friends. We have set up progressive dinners that included a garden tour at each participant's home. One family served cocktails, another appetizers, the third, salad or soup, the fourth, the main course, the fifth, dessert and coffee. We saw a Japanese-style garden, a terraced garden, a rock-and-woodland garden, an English garden, a water garden. What a pleasant way to spend a portion of a day!

"The very act of tending a garden can be meditative."

Letting Go

A FLOWER GARDEN IS A PLACE THAT IS MOST DEEPLY
REWARDING when you are willing to relinquish some
control in its planting and tending. Your garden will be
most generous with you when you allow it to create its
own expression amid your handiwork.

I cannot count the times when my garden has
surprised me with gifts. I have planted something that
I thought would be just perfect, only to have the plant
wither and die. Before I replaced it, however, my garden
had provided its own substitute – some lovely little
wildflower for me to look at and enjoy.

I even have been pleasantly surprised by the
appearance of a cherry tomato plant or an errant squash
vine with its giant leaves magically produced from
compost. These volunteers made their way amid my herb
garden, chrysanthemum, and hollyhocks. After considering
pulling out these visitors, I decided to let them remain
to most pleasant effect, as they soon would lace their

way through my carefully planned garden space. They trailed out onto the lawn, lending an uncontrolled and marvelously lush appearance to the garden.

Or I have put in several new plants, only to find that they rapidly outgrew their space and I had to transplant them. The richness of the soil and the plenitude of the sun have swelled my plants with health and fullness, so that I always am rearranging them. If I were to give my garden a little freedom, it would conspire with me in a sculptural design that would constantly recast and renew itself.

A garden, particularly if it is well tended, forces you to stop and observe. It is easy to live too much in our heads or to be sucked into a mill of constant activity that leaves no room for quiet, for meditation, for reflection. In observation can be release. When we stop truly to look, to take in what we see, we open ourselves to the essence of another life. It causes us to still ourselves while we accept the reality of something larger. By letting go of ourselves, we find a moment of freedom and often delight. A garden provides many occasions for observation and contemplation.

The very act of tending a garden can be meditative. The repetition of planting seeds, of pulling weeds, or of cutting back dead branches and blooms, can produce a freeing of the mind while we are, at the same time, fully grounded in the earth.

In tending a garden, it is helpful to accept that much is not under our control. The growing months can bring overly dry and hot weather or overly wet and cold conditions. There may be an oversupply of pesky insects and an undersupply of birds or bees. We might have violent storms that damage our gardens, or our neighbors' pets or farm animals might take a destructive liking to our gardens.

One year we hardly could keep ourselves in tomatoes, though we had numerous plants and a good crop. We couldn't figure out what was happening to these vegetables. Then one day we discovered – too late – that our neighbor's chickens loved tomatoes. When we weren't around, the chickens would wander down to the vegetable garden below and help themselves. Or there was the time that a neighbor's horse got loose in our yard and threatened to trample everything.

It does little good to drive ourselves wild trying to fight nature and happenstance. I have been down that road, and it is full of much added work and frustration. We can try to do what we can to assure the survival of our beloved plants. For myself, however, I have found it best not to take this too far, so that I don't turn my delight in gardening into a prescription for misery.

Rachel Carson, in *The Silent Spring*, saw it another way. "The 'control of nature,'" she said, "is a phrase conceived in arrogance...."

The potential applications of this philosophy to everyday life are many. We can hold too tightly to how we want things to be and miss the surprises and the learning that can come when we embrace the virtue of letting go.

"Simply by looking, we can
feel part of something larger
than ourselves, something that
carries the mysteries of beauty
and change, and lessons about
the nature of life."

Winter Snows

IT WAS A SATURDAY. On this winter day, the snow was
gone, but sunshine had come to take its place. In Ohio,
the appearance of sun in winter is rather like the good
fortune of snow. I had become accustomed to grey, winter
days, but it was a special joy to experience sunshine on a
weekend when I could be at home. Just as when it snowed,
I felt compelled to run outside and soak up the sun before
cloudy skies overtook it. I would look for any excuse to be
outside, but on snow-free winter days, a walk was the most
common one I used.

So George and I donned our jackets. We walked
past our brown and dormant garden and set off toward
a neighbor's land. We crossed an old soybean field, the
stumpy stalks of the cut plants breaking under the soles of
our hiking boots, walked to the top of the low hill where we
could see for miles, then descended to another neighbor's
land. We walked winding paths laced with leftover snow,
the wet beginnings of thawing earth, the footprints of deer,

and dried field flowers – mostly goldenrod, brown now and leaning toward earth. I felt the sun on my face and the coolness of air brushed by a light wind.

We made our way to yet another property maybe a half-mile from our home. The neighbor has a house on acres of rolling fields with young trees at the center. It is especially beautiful land here, hilly, with a mixture of trees, shrubs, and open, grassy areas. Our neighbor had erected a small cabin at the back of his acres, where he could go, sit beside his wood stove, and enjoy this land he loves so much. It was his retirement gift to himself. We had stopped by regularly when he was planning and building the cabin, and he proudly showed us his progress. He was like a child building his first clubhouse. His eyes sparkled with excitement. He could hardly wait for his cabin to be done, the cabin that would put him closer to his land.

I understand our neighbor's passion for this place. In truth we all are especially blessed if this bit of earth we find ourselves on is graced with grass, trees, flowers, and a little wildlife. For me this is especially true if it has a view of nature uninterrupted by a density of buildings and concrete. Then our spirit is refreshed just by the presence of it. Simply by looking, we can feel part of something larger than ourselves, something that carries the mysteries of beauty and change, and lessons about the nature of life.

*   *   *

This was the last weekend of my fifty-sixth year. I had decided that this long, holiday weekend would be mine to spend as I pleased. I lost most of the previous day to not feeling well. But this particular morning, I had set out after a good night's rest to get the last little bit out of the inch of snow resting sparingly on our land. Someone from Michigan or the far West would have laughed at the conditions under which I skied today, but I was happy even for this pitifully thin coating of snow and ice over the frozen grass and earth. I managed an hour of skating on barely more than snow vapors. The best ski was down our long, blacktopped driveway. A veneer of undisturbed snow turned out to be an excellent skating surface.

I went inside to find that former barn cat Max, who belonged now to our neighbors with the goats, was stretched out asleep on the dining room chair. I fixed a cup of hot tea and enjoyed the white-dusted landscape, the dried leavings of my garden now coated with fairy dust, and the distant frozen surface of our pond with its dried cattails.

Across the street, cows huddled beside the bales of hay left for them to eat by the old farmer who lived for these creatures. This was especially true since his wife passed away a couple of years before. These fine, fat Black Angus cattle were his pride and joy, and he treated them well. They roamed rolling, green meadows and cooled themselves in summer under a row of trees partway up the hill and in a pond dug especially for them. These cows had a good life, and their young played exuberantly by their mothers' sides. The old farmer even had let a fawn, whose mother had been killed, stay among the cows that had taken it in. For months it had frolicked with the young calves and had been mothered by the herd. But one day the fawn was gone. None of us ever knew whether it just left, whether the herd had pushed it out, or whether it had been killed by a hunter or a car. One day it simply was gone. It seemed that the old farmer missed that fawn, as did the passengers in the cars that used to stop in the roadway to observe this phenomenon. I knew I did.

*　　*　　*

This morning we skied. George and I took our cross-country skis in the back of the truck and traveled the short distance to our neighbors' twenty-acre field. A thin layer of snow over the grasses made a good skiing surface, and the hills on their lot made for pleasurable runs. Their field was dotted with tender starts of trees our neighbors had planted this year and last and was swirled with the brown forms of bushes between young trees on their hillock stretching between woods and farmers' fields. Our neighbors were kind to encourage us to use their land. They loved when we walked, skied, and ran on it. The snow this morning was dimpled with rabbit and deer tracks and was otherwise undisturbed, except for tire marks from our neighbors' car.

In a while, George tired and headed for home. I stayed behind, reveling in being able to stay outside in the cold without getting chilled. My body was warm and wet from exertion. I hardly noticed the bite of the wind. I gazed up at the small, west-facing cabin our neighbor had built last year on the top of the hill, as I slid up and down the lower part with my skis. Flocks of birds circled in the cloudy sky. They changed direction and came to rest in the tall trees edging a nearby farmer's field. Cold hung white in the air from the breath leaving my nostrils, and I set off for one more run through this land our neighbors so disarmingly loved.

And then I saw it – coyote tracks in the snow. I hadn't known we had coyotes in this area, until George had skied here last week and had spotted a large one crossing the soybean field beside this neighbor's property. It was then that our neighbor had confirmed to George that coyotes frequent this area – grey ones, reddish ones, and even a white coyote. Suddenly the coyotes' scat and paw prints I'd witnessed over time and couldn't identify were beginning to make sense to me. I had never seen a coyote by day, as George did last week, and only one time saw one by night. It was on a Western backpacking trip, high up in the mountains. It was a magical sight then and a pleasure now to think of these creatures roaming at night so close to our home and garden.

"The repetition, the silence, the grounding and freedom of the earth, all of these still the mind and refresh the spirit."

On Solitude

GARDENS CAN PROVIDE US WITH AN EXCUSE TO
BE ALONE. It is a challenge to find time apart from
our families, our jobs, and the demands of other
responsibilities. Erica Jong said that solitude is un-
American. Ralph Waldo Emerson wrote, "Solitude is
impractical, and society fatal. We must keep our head in
the one and our hands in the other." Amelia Barr noted,
"…solitude is such a potential thing. We hear voices in
solitude, [sic] we never hear in the hurry and turmoil of
life; we receive counsels and comforts, [sic] we get under
no other condition.…"

A degree of solitude is essential to tap and renew
ourselves through our own inner wellsprings.

Working in my garden is, for me, a form of
meditation. The repetition, the silence, the grounding and
freedom of the earth, all of these still my mind and refresh
my spirit. At least when the weather is hospitable, I can
find some solitude by tending my garden.

I find that guilt often keeps me from solitude. The demands of my work schedule give me too little time at home. I feel compelled to spend most of this precious time with my husband and taking care of our home needs. And then there are volunteering and other family responsibilities. All of these demands can leave very little temporal space for solitude.

I think that without solitude, we can lose touch with who we are. We become that employee and this wife, daughter, parent, and friend, but we can cease to remember who we are, all by ourselves. We can forget to dream if we have no solitude. How can we create without solitude? Yet it can be the last on our list of imperatives as we struggle through the demands of our days. Everything and everyone calls for our attention. But somehow we can fail to hear our own tiny voice, calling from deep inside ourselves, imploring us to take a little time to be still, to listen, to dream.

What failings of modern life have made it so difficult to acknowledge that small voice and choose it, at least for a while each day, over the other responsibilities that beckon to us? We may have learned how to sacrifice for others – as well we should. What is tragically hard to learn, however, is how to sacrifice the demands of others for the requirements of our own inner selves. It can seem a selfish decision, and therefore wrong. But what will we have to give to others if we don't nourish our soul with a little solitude? Or as Walter Savage Landor wrote, "… solitude is the audience-chamber of God."

My garden has made my choice less burdensome. Gardening adds quality – beauty – to my family's, friends', and neighbors' lives. By working in my garden, I can enrich others' experience while nurturing my own. I can find solitude there, without the guilt. But we ought not to have to bargain for the right to feed our souls. We ought only to have to say that our soul has its season too – and this is its rightful time.

"In winter, a garden sleeps."

The Sleeping Garden

IN WINTER, A GARDEN SLEEPS. It pulls up its blanket of snow and frozen soil, and beds down for a long period of hibernation.

Bushes, trees, and flowering plants drop their leaves and become skeletons reaching up and out to some future time when they will shake their bones and dress themselves in the flesh of new, green life.

They will don bonnets of showy flowers and capes of verdant leaves as they dash out to meet spring with its roaring sunshine and chattering rain.

"Spring is an offering of discovery, biting at the tail of winter's long memory."

The Freedom of Spring

WINTER FADED UNCHARACTERISTICALLY GENTLY INTO SPRING this year. Cold spring rains replaced winter snows, and bulbs rose out of the ground and proclaimed winter over.

Spring brought with it that special sense of freedom. No longer were we housebound. We could move about as we pleased without the limitations of the cold. Quite suddenly the world seemed larger, and the warming air and the beginnings of a garden rising from last year's dead stalks beckoned.

Birds were returning, robins being the most noticeable among them. Robins always have struck me as such strong and confident creatures. They hop about with very little regard for you as they search for worms. And they display a clear sense of pleasure with themselves and the activity in which they're engaged.

That can change, however, with motherhood. A female robin built a nest this year on a downspout elbow beside our well-developed Sweet Autumn Clematis vine that borders our patio. I was surprised at how small and how lacking in sturdiness her nest appeared to be. The impression grew stronger when I saw it become the home of not only the mother robin, but three ever-hungry babies. I couldn't imagine how they all could fit there. Because the clematis – and the nest – were less than a dozen feet from our sliding patio door, the mother felt compelled to fly off every time we went in or out. Since this occurred often, the mother was very busy between her efforts to draw attention away from the nest and her search for more food to feed her young.

If I was very quiet when the mother was away on one of her hunting rounds, I could see the baby robins' three little heads with their beaks pointed upward, ready to catch the worms that their mother surely would bring. I kept a close eye on the nest, hoping to catch the moment when the babies would attempt to fly. But one day all four robins simply were gone, the nest abandoned. As spring progressed into summer, the clematis and hollyhocks grew high and thick, obscuring the nest – but I long would remember its lively contents.

Spring brings all kinds of fresh life and newfound activity. Spring is an offering of discovery, biting at the tail of winter's long memory.

"There can be a certain beauty
in being overdone."

The Fullness of Summer

ALTHOUGH WE WERE WELL INTO JULY, the rains of
spring continued. The browns that usually crept into the
lawn and garden were absent. Everything, everywhere, was
green and lush.

My garden had become so overgrown that I didn't
know where to begin to thin it. But when I shed my sense
of obligation to at least a little control and made myself
look at it from the vantage point of a more detached
individual, I had to say that I rather liked the obscenity of
my garden's growing pulchritude.

There can be a certain beauty in being overdone.
Gigantic armfuls of pink yarrow, yellow daylily, white-
flowering oregano, and black-eyed Susan spilled out over
the patio and onto the lawn. Tomato plants were springing
up everywhere – amid my hollyhocks, under the purple
coneflower, among my irises, between the zinnias. I came
to like this elaborate potpourri of planned and unplanned
life, and decided to stop fretting and just enjoy the

abundance we were experiencing for the gift that it was.

I remember a particular day in mid-July, when it was an unseasonable seventy degrees and all the humidity of the past weeks of heavy rains and flooding had lifted from the air. It was breezy, as occasional passing storms rolled around on the periphery. The storms never descended on us, though, and the day drifted in and out of sunshine.

I took advantage of the wet soil to try to liberate my horribly overgrown vegetable garden. I scarcely could find my pepper and basil plants for all the weeds. They even had dwarfed some of the normally strong tomato plants. For weeks I had neglected my vegetables for my flowers, and I was feeling a bit remiss in my duties. It took hours of hard work to rid my vegetables of the worst of the weeds, and I could have spent that much time again to finish the job. I chose, however, not to let my guilt get the better of me and to give myself time for other chores and for enjoyment of the day.

It strikes me, at times, that I spend so very much more time gardening than I do sitting back and savoring the results. But then I remember my joy in the activity and in the sense of discovery when I unearthed my zinnias from weeds and found the first bloom of the summer – a strident, red zinnia blossom spread out like a monarch's crown, facing up and just waiting to be admired. And at that moment, I had to admit that gardening's hard, sweaty, physical work also carries the pleasure of really knowing your plants and of helping them to grow strong and beautiful. Being a gardener indeed can be a lot like being a parent.

"As the black raspberries came on, small and wild and full of thorns, he would go down each morning and pick them by the half-quart and later the quart. He would come back up to the house, his hands scratched, but his face triumphant with the victory of the sweet berries."

Switchgrass, Vegetables, and Other Sources of Sustenance

GEORGE TALKED CONSTANTLY FOR A TIME ABOUT THE WONDERS of switchgrass. It was as if he had discovered the Holy Grail. Well perhaps it was if you wanted to help save the Earth – or if you happened to be a buffalo.

Many, many moons ago, America's heartland was covered with mile upon mile of switchgrass. It was a mainstay of the North American bison diet and a rich source of nutrients for the earth. Settlers burned and cleared it, however, to make way for farmland, and eventually its name all but fell from our common vocabulary.

Everyone's except for George's that is. There were days when I thought it was the only word that George knew. That is until asparagus started to pop up around the field behind our house and the vegetable garden began to bear fruit.

Each year in the past, I tried as best I could to juggle my job with my house and family responsibilities –

and tending the vegetable garden in addition to my flower beds. I never was able to do the vegetable garden justice, as any time I had, I longed to work among my flowers.
But this year George agreed to take on the vegetable garden. I bought plants and seeds for him, and we planted them together. George, however, would be the one to tend them throughout the growing season. I breathed a sigh of relief. What I didn't expect, however, was with how much gusto he would take on the task.

George always is one to find the most practical and efficient solution to any effort. I always have admired that about him. He put old carpet between the rows to keep the weeds down. He fertilized liberally. He set up a sprinkler system that was fed by the pond some thirty feet away. He established little nurseries in large pots after moles consumed his bean seeds and grew in the pots green beans and basil from seed, as well as cilantro and spinach.

In previous years, I generally planted eight or ten tomato plants of various types and seven or eight pepper plants of different varieties. In addition, I put in green beans and herbs – basil and cilantro in particular – and occasionally leaf lettuce or spinach and a single zucchini or yellow squash plant. But this year we had all of these, in addition to kale, Swiss chard, two zucchini plants, and eggplant.

The growing of food, however, did not end with the vegetable garden. George began separating previously producing asparagus volunteers from our field and planting them along the fence line. Every day he would walk the field, picking ready asparagus spears, harvesting several a day during the height of the season and at least three or four on less productive days. We could eat asparagus every day for two or three months – imagine that!

Numerous tomato plant volunteers sprang up in both the vegetable and flower gardens. George dutifully planted most of the volunteers around downed tree stumps and along the fence line not far from the asparagus transplants. We were set to have tomatoes in abundance!

Now that George saw the possibility of vegetable self-sufficiency, he looked to the fruit options on our land. The first to produce were the mulberry trees. In truth, we'd never viewed these trees as a source of human sustenance. When we picked and ate a few here and there, we would remark on the watery and rather bland nature of the fruit. In the past, mulberries mostly had been something we wiped off the bottoms of our shoes before entering the house – or cleaned up the remains left by birds on our cars, lawn furniture, and windows. These berries were a nuisance for humans, and food for birds and other animals. We tolerated them, but had little use for them. Until George remembered that there was such a thing as mulberry wine.

"Do you have a recipe for mulberry wine?" he asked one day. I went through my crowded bookshelves and came up with an old book about winemaking that I'd bought thirty years before. I consulted the index and turned to a page with a recipe for the brew.

It was quite simple really – water, sugar, mulberries, and yeast…a little boiling and sieving, followed by fermenting, and finally bottling and corking…a little time and a little care to not mingle any "bad bacteria" with the "good bacteria," as the recipe cautioned. But after just two weeks in a tightly covered pot and prior to the bottling and resting part of the process, we tasted the first of our first-ever bottle of homemade wine. And lo and behold, it actually was rather good – and very strong. Homemade wine, a friend informed us, can be twice or more as high in alcohol content as store-bought wine. It has quite a kick!

Now George was hooked. Imagine making wine so easily and cheaply – less than a dollar a bottle! George thought of the other fruit on our land that either was about to ripen or that would later in the season: raspberries, blackberries, apples, and pears. All could be made into wine! George was ecstatic.

But as the black raspberries came on, small and wild and full of thorns, he would go down each morning and pick them by the half-quart and later the quart. He would come back up to the house, his hands scratched, but his face triumphant with the victory of the sweet berries that we'd ladle over our yogurt, oatmeal, and ice cream. Between the difficulty of picking the raspberries and the pleasure of eating them, George decided that taking quarts of them to make wine seemed a poor use of these small, dark treasures. So we ate what we could and froze the rest, to enjoy over the coming months when fresh raspberries were just a memory.

In time, there were fewer and fewer raspberries to pick, and the blackberry bushes started to produce. They were not as sweet as the raspberries at first, but they were larger and satisfying in a plumper, slightly more tart way. Our blackberry bushes were nowhere near as prolific, however, and their thorns were more formidable. But George could not pass up fruit sitting there just waiting to be devoured.

And so the summer passed as we struggled to use the mountain of kale eight plants produced and the huge zucchinis from just two plants, let alone the pounds and pounds of tomatoes so many tomato plants would generate. It was impossible to imagine how two people could use so much produce! I joked with him about taking the vegetables to the farmers' market in town – or selling them to the farm stand down the road. But I knew we just would give away what we couldn't eat.

There is a certain primal pleasure in growing and harvesting your own food. Returning to the land, whether for food or for beauty, has real and abundant rewards.

"I think of my mother and my childhood every time I cut lilacs and hydrangeas and place them in her dusty-purple vase."

Gardens of the Past

WHEN I GARDEN, I THINK OF MY MOTHER. She was
wonderful at growing flowers. She used to spend in the
garden whatever time was not needed for her house, her
husband, and her two growing children. She was especially
fond of pansies, violets, hollyhocks, roses, lilacs, and
hydrangeas. Her wedding corsage, she once told me, was
made of pansies. "I have always loved them," she said.

She was much more skilled and had better luck with
her roses than I. I especially remember her Peace rose – a
magnificent plant with glossy, deep green leaves and large,
exquisite blooms in the delicate shades of dawn's glowing
yellows and pinks. I think I have never seen roses more
beautiful than my mother's. Once in a while, she would
cut an opening bud and bring it inside for the dining
room table or for the living room. I would stare at it in
fascination. So much beauty in a single bloom.

She also loved to pick numerous long stalks of old-
fashioned lilacs from the large bush beside the kitchen

door – or the massive blue-lavender hydrangeas that grew along the east side of our house on Long Island. She would bring them in and deposit them in a large, lovely, lavender-and-blue pottery vase my great aunt had bought in Jamaica many years before. I always loved that vase. My mother gave it to me a few years ago. I think of her and my childhood every time I cut lilacs and hydrangeas and place them in that dusty-purple vase. I even have planted these flowers in the hope of emulating that aesthetic experience from my childhood.

The peonies in my garden are there because my sister, who passed away some years ago, adored them. As a young teenager, my sister always used to walk by the house of a woman who had dozens of the plants in a long row a few feet from her white picket fence. The stalks would be bent to the ground with the weight of the lovely blooms. Not able to resist not knowing what these flowers were any longer, my sister, Judy, walked up to the woman's front door. She knocked, and when the door opened, Judy introduced herself and asked the flowers' name. The woman was kind, and she answered Judy's query. Seeing how much my sister loved the flowers, the woman excused herself, grabbed her shears, and proceeded to cut an armload of white and pink peonies for her. Judy came home, grinning from ear to ear. I don't think I ever saw her happier as a child than at that moment. And so I planted white and pink peonies, in memory of my sister.

"It is part of the mystery
of gardens – and life – that you
never know what to expect,
despite your study and your
plans. Life will deliver to you
its own promise."

Fall Again
The last days of fall are blowing toward winter.

THE SUN STREAMED THROUGH THE WILDLY BLOWING LEAVES of the trees. Gold and red tumbled over the green grass and fallen pine needles. It was time to cut back the dead flowers, put away the flowerpots and lawn chairs, and clear the vegetable garden.

I blissfully hacked away at the dried stalks of lilies and purple coneflower, black-eyed Susan, chrysanthemum, daisy, and hollyhock plants. I gathered seeds from old favorites in the garden and labeled them for spring planting.

A praying mantis clung to the warmth of the bricks on the outside of the house between the sliding patio door and the grill. I wondered what would happen to him when winter came. Shooing Max, the neighbor's cat, away from the praying mantis, I watched Max jump up on George's tractor and stare at me a while before washing himself down with his tongue.

The first days of November brought chilly weather and alternately, sunshine and dark, forbidding skies.

* * *

The expectation had been that temperatures would drop into the thirties, below seasonal norms. Light snow flurries were predicted. It was still green outside, however. Lush grass extended my view of the front yard from my vantage point inside the house where I was working. The verdant grasses picked up again on the other side of our country road. There, fat rolls of hay nestled against one another in front of the red clapboard barn. The neighbor's cows were lying in the grass beside the barn and under the bare trees that waited for winter. The sky hovered above them, grey, moist, and filled with a light wind that rattled the denuded tree branches and shimmied among the sharp, green yucca leaves outside our front windows.

Nearly all the flowers in my garden were brown, dry, and even black from frosty nights and mornings. A few surprises in addition to the green grass, however, lit up the landscape of our yard. The purple and white alyssum – such delicate, tiny flowers – had proven astonishingly resilient to the cold that had set in during the past weeks. These plants not only had continued to bloom, they seemed almost to have become richer in color. Perhaps it was the brownness of the rest of the garden that made the purples so bright, the whites so pure – as the sometimes drabness of life that can set off a vivid moment.

The lavendar yarrow had made a comeback. When it had looked spent, I had cut it back, only to see stalks shoot up and flower again. More than a dozen large yarrow blooms lined the patio outside our sliding glass door. While most of the chrysanthemum plants had faded and dried, near the front door purple ones lingered, somewhat spoiled by time. But just off the crest of the hill on which our house sits, in a small garden I cleared on the hillside two years ago, was a late-blooming mum with large, daisylike, cream-colored blooms. The heavy blossoms bent the stalks to the ground and onto the branches of a nearby shrub.

*　　*　　*

Life's parallels to gardening are legion. You work hard in spring, clearing winter debris, preparing the soil, sowing seeds, planting starts, all in the hope of harvesting beauty at some unknown point in time. You dream of a little beauty…to awaken the heart, delight the spirit, and stir the soul. And if you are lucky, you will be rewarded for your work. You never can predict the nature of your rewards – or your failures. It is part of the mystery of gardens – and life – that you never know what to expect, despite your study and your plans. Life will deliver to you its own promise.

"Your garden is just a step or a glance away. It is nature's treasure, right outside your door."

Gardens and Wilderness

I HAVE SPENT DECADES EXPLORING WILDERNESS and decades gardening. They both provide dazzling displays of nature. They can put you in touch with the wonders of the Earth and the mysteries of the ages. But they are not at all the same.

With wilderness, the work is in getting there. Once there, you have only to take in and savor the moment. There are no dead blossoms to pick, no weeds to pull, no overgrown bushes to transplant, no dry roots to water.

Wilderness just is. It radiates beauty in its untouched form. No one has tamed it. No one owns or sculpts it. You love it or you don't. You see its secret or brazen beauty – or you don't.

Gardens, however, don't just happen. They are the result of some planning and are the creative expression of an individual. They can be free in form or tightly controlled. They can make room for the unexpected – a wildflower or a volunteer from the previous year. Or they can be firmly fashioned to a plan. They are the reflection of a person's character and the individual's personal philosophy of life. And importantly, your garden is just a step or a glance away. It is nature's treasure, right outside your door.

"Mixing annuals with perennials
provides the perfect mix of
constancy and fluctuation that I
so love in a garden."

Gardens and Lifestyles

I NEVER HAVE MADE A FORMAL STUDY of whether or not gardens parallel people's lifestyles, but I suspect they do.

Always I have liked an element of the unpredictable in life – and I must say I love a garden that is not overly repetitive and that rambles a bit. I don't like tidy rows. I like winding garden lines and a free-form look. I like a mixture of colors, textures, shapes, a variety of flowers, shrubs, trees, and levels. I like rocks in and bordering my garden. I like a garden that always is changing. I would not care for a garden of only annuals – those hearty, energetic plants that bloom their hearts out all summer. Predictably. They are wonderful to punctuate a perennial garden, but there is nothing, to my mind, to replace the artfulness of perennials.

If you time perennials properly, you can create a pattern of color in your garden throughout the blooming season. Perennials come in waves: first the spring bulbs, followed by forget-me-not, Vinca, lilacs, irises, early-blooming sage and peonies, yarrow, and soon clematis, yucca, roses, early daisies, and early lilies. The wave rolls on to hostas, the early-blooming daisy-mums, the later-blooming sage, the daylilies, hydrangeas, blooming herbs, hollyhocks, black-eyed Susan, summer daisies and purple coneflower. Finally we are left with sedum, the Sweet Autumn Clematis, the hearty yarrow, a second round of purple coneflower, chrysanthemum, a late blooming of the rose, and if you're lucky, a re-blooming of the earlier-season clematis and daylily.

I like to intersperse annuals among my perennials to assure a certain sturdiness and constancy of color. First come the pansies, then the alyssum, petunia, geranium, impatiens, snapdragon, marigold, Melampodium, an assortment of zinnias and daisies, including the Gloriosa Daisy. I buy the showy, pink-blooming Mandevilla vine for the patio and pot hibiscus bushes for bright splashes of their coral-red or yellow blooms and their dark green, glossy leaves. I hang planters on poles here and there in the garden, wherever the accent of height plays well. I propagate trailing plants for the flowerpots, because they give grace and subtlety to the display.

Mixing annuals with perennials, then, provides the perfect mix of constancy and fluctuation that I so love in a garden.

My garden is full of change, as is my life. They both are loaded with activity. Mine is not a simple garden and mirrors my love of complexity. It isn't easy to maintain either, and I ponder that. With such a busy life, I should find ways to simplify the caretaking, but I seem not to be able to resist the plantings that cause the most work.

Always, my garden fosters unexpected additions. I allow little weeds here and there that have a certain grace. I frequently leave the volunteer tomato, squash, or cilantro plants or marigold, yarrow, or forget-me-not. I love the unplanned nature of some of these garden visitors and can't imagine destroying them.

This gets me into trouble. I hate to kill a perfectly fine and useful plant – or its seeds. I wind up with many more volunteers than I can use, and I quickly run out of places to transplant them. There's something about killing a useful life that bothers me. This makes a lot of work for me, however, and I often end up disposing of the plants anyway, by virtue of having nowhere to place them.

I do believe that your personality and the style with which you live your life are very much evident in your garden. This is one of the things I love about looking at the plantings of others. I can see parts of who they are poured out into the nature of how they have designed and tended their plants. I understand their ability to imagine and to realize their dreams and all the hard work that stands between the point of imagining and the place of realization.

"When I am troubled or
lack serenity, when the press of
the world gets too great,
I want more than ever to be in
my garden with my hands dug
into the soil."

The Peace of Gardens

IN THE MORNING, THE FIRST THING I LOOK AT, after my husband, is my garden. I awake with anticipation. What new seedling has sprouted? What new flower opened? Will my garden be fresh from the night's rain or the morning dew? Will it be bathed in sun or shadowed by clouds? Will the insects or birds be busy yet? What will I find?

It refreshes me, just to look at my garden.

When I am troubled or lack serenity, when the press of the world gets too great, I want more than ever to be in my garden with my hands dug into the soil. There I find solace, a place to shut out the world for a while and immerse myself in beauty. Beauty elevates the spirit, takes you outside yourself, makes you appreciate what's around you. Suddenly the world – and your problems – looks more manageable.

"In winter, the soul stirs – not from what's without, but from what lies within."

The Seasons Turn Again to Winter

THERE IS NOTHING GRADUAL ABOUT WINTER. It is a shock to the system, like the presence of death.

Winter brings a firm conclusion to the world outside as you knew it. Much of the life you observed over the rest of the year has fled, died, or has begun a lengthy period of hibernation. People and their pets retreat indoors. So, often, does your spirit, which can retreat to more solitary and introspective activities. This is a good thing, I believe, as it can be a time for your spiritual seed to germinate and find nourishment for a new beginning in spring.

It also is a time for a greater consciousness of form. It is in winter that you best can see the form of your garden and of trees, shrubs, and the landscape as a whole. That view in the distance that had been veiled by greenery, suddenly now shows itself with its rises and dips and in the subtlety of its form. It is a time, as well, that you have a heightened awareness of the form of your own life. There are few places to escape to in winter. You find yourself looking back at yourself, which can lead to healthy contemplation, reflection, and inner growth.

As in winter your garden gathers strength for the coming spring, so you too can gain nourishment through relief from many of your outdoor diversions. You acquire time and space to become more aware of your own inner form and its substance. In winter, the soul stirs – not from what's without, but from what lies within. It is a time of preparation, when the body may rest, but the mind and spirit get increasingly busy.

The change of seasons provides a certain balance to your life. It forces you to refocus your energies and to learn different lessons. When spring comes, you may find yourself receptive in new ways to the teachings of a garden.

"I often feel most thankful
for my daily life when I'm
in my garden among the richly
varied and intricate plants
that I so love."

The Gift of Gardens

IT SEEMS TO ME THAT OUR LIVES WOULD BE SMALLER if we had no gardens. It is not by chance that the Biblical history of mankind began in a garden: it is where human beings were planted in order for their spirits to be nourished and grow.

I often feel most thankful for my daily life when I'm in my garden among the richly varied and intricate plants that I so love. Here I have freedom to explore an honest experience of the fullness of being.

Gardens can be an invitation to engage in the mysteries of nature. They are places where divine and human creativity meet. They are the manifestation of life born of a powerful mixture of urgency, devotion, delicacy, love, birth, death, and transcendent beauty.

"There is the sense that the land you helped to bloom and your hands etched with dirt share at once the pulse of the stars and the form and gritty substance of Earth."

And at the End of the Day

IT'S THE END OF THE DAY. The work of gardening is
done, the sun is setting crimson behind the trees, and
a rosy glow brushes the surface of the pond. You look
at the flowers that have absorbed the sun's now gentle
luminescence and know why gardens stir the soul.

There is the sense that the land you helped to
bloom and your hands etched with dirt share at once the
pulse of the stars and the form and gritty substance of
Earth. You look out at a day ending amid the last throws
of sunlight, exhaling into the western horizon and bathing
in gold the field to the east that is vibrant with anticipation
under the moon rising. You feel the primal pull and know
that you and what you have worked for and cherished are
part of a grand web of life. From earth and desire have
sprung something of beauty to nourish and link the spirit
to the heavens and the waiting stars.

Thanks to fellow writers Joe Aiello,
David Farrell, and Larry Budenz for
their unfailing support and constructive
criticism – and to Ben Logan,
Ani Hurwitz, and Bob Bingenheimer
for their help and encouragement.

2382438R00052

Printed in Great Britain
by Amazon.co.uk, Ltd.,
Marston Gate.